Engineering a Win

Stephanie Loureiro

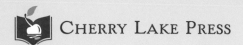

Published in the United States of America by Cherry Lake Publishing Group
Ann Arbor, Michigan
www.cherrylakepublishing.com

Reading Adviser: Beth Walker Gambro, MS, Ed., Reading Consultant, Yorkville, IL

Photo Credits: Cover: ©Gino Santa Maria / Shutterstock; ©tharrison / Getty Images; © RobinOlimb / Getty Images; ©JuliarStudio / Getty Images; ©checha / Getty Images; page 7: ©Jessica Orozco; page 8: ©Jessica Orozco; page 9: ©drvector / Shutterstock; page 10: ©Jessica Orozco; page 11: ©Jessica Orozco; page 12: ©Photoplotnikov / Getty Images; page 12: ©LeoPride / Getty Images; page 12: ©setory / Getty Images; page 14: ©Kirill Nesmelov / Getty Images; page 15: ©pikepicture / Shutterstock; page 16: ©RichLegg / Getty Images; page 17: ©lioputra / Getty Images; page 17: ©lioputra / Getty Images; page 17: ©Michal Sanca / Shutterstock; page 19: ©bor-zebra / Getty Images; page 20: ©higyou / Getty Images; page 21: ©Andrew_Rybalko / Getty Images; page 23: ©Mack15 / Getty Images; page 23: © / Getty Images; page 24: ©Jessica Orozco; page 24: ©Amin Yusifov / Getty Images; page 26: ©winui / Shutterstock; page 27: ©Jessica Orozco; page 27: ©alphabetMN / Getty Images; page 28: ©Jessica Orozco

Cherry Lake Press is an imprint of Cherry Lake Publishing Group.

Library of Congress Cataloging-in-Publication Data
Library of Congress Cataloging-in-Publication Data has been filed and is available at catalog.loc.gov.

Cherry Lake Publishing Group would like to acknowledge the work of the Partnership for 21st Century Learning, a Network of Battelle for Kids. Please visit http://www.battelleforkids.org/networks/p21 for more information.

Printed in the United States of America

Note from publisher: Websites change regularly, and their future contents are outside of our control. Supervise children when conducting any recommended online searches for extended learning opportunities.

Stephanie Loureiro is a writer and editor. She's been writing since she was nine years old and loves working on books that help kids discover things they love. When she's not writing, she can be found curled up reading a book, doing Olympic weightlifting, or singing loudly and dancing around to Taylor Swift. She currently lives in Idaho with her husband, daughter, and two dogs.

CONTENTS

Introduction
Better Tech, Better Performance | 4

Chapter 1
Engineered Equipment | 6

Chapter 2
Better Bodies | 12

Chapter 3
Engineered Environments | 18

Chapter 4
Wonders of Engineering | 22

Activity | 30
Learn More | 31
Glossary | 32
Index | 32

Better Tech, Better Performance

Competitive sports have been around for hundreds of years. Many sports have had the same goals and rules since they first started. But some things have changed. Technology has made sports even better. It has helped athletes perform better. Athletes now have better uniforms and equipment. They also have new and better ways of training. These changes are thanks to engineering. Engineering is solving problems by using science and math.

Timeline of Sports Tech

1954: SHOT CLOCK
The National Basketball Association (NBA) introduces the 24-second shot clock. There is a swift increase of 14 Points per game (PPG). More scoring makes games more exciting.

1980: COMPOSITE RACKETS
Composite rackets are lighter and sturdier than wood ones. These larger rackets give players better control and harder hitting power.

1990: TITANIUM CLUBS
Titanium is a type of lightweight metal. In 1990, driver clubs were first made of titanium. Titanium driver clubs allow for a larger sweet spot. Golfers have a faster swing, too.

1994: IN-HELMET HEADSETS
In-helmet headsets allow coaches and quarterbacks to talk. Now game play adjustments can be made in a moment's notice.

2000: LZR SWIMSUIT
The Speedo LZR Racer suit is made of high-tech fabric. It reduces drag and water resistance. It was banned from the Olympic Games because it helps swimmers too much.

2012: NEW HELMETS
Concussion helmets reduce the chances of players getting concussions if they are hit by a ball. The 2012 upgrade works against ball speeds up to 100 miles (161 km) per hour.

2013, Complex

CHAPTER 1

Engineered Equipment

Technology in sports may seem like a new idea. But it has been a part of sports since the 1920s. It began to play a bigger role in the 1950s and 1960s. Changes were made to clothing and equipment. Billions of dollars are spent on sports equipment each year.

Players and teams want the best tech. It helps them play better. This drives new innovations. Video technology is one of these. Virtual imaging is another. There are even new devices that track time to help athletes. All of this equipment-based engineering can lead to more wins!

Smart Sport Tech

Smart sports equipment uses technology. Tracking devices are an example. There are even smart balls with sensors in them. The National Football League (NFL) began using smart tech in 2013. It started using motion sensors. They help track information during games and practices.

WHAT	WHO
motion sensors	Zebra MotionWorks Sports Solutions

WHEN	WHY
first used during the 2013 NFL season	to track information; where a player is on the field, how fast a player runs, how close a player gets to another

HOW

Sensors are placed around the stadium. Small sensors are built into the player's shoulder pads. The sensors can pinpoint the location of a player on the field. They can tell where a player is within 6 inches (15 centimeters)!

2022, Zebra

Football Helmet History

In some sports, there is a high risk for injuries. Football players are often tackled. Players need to be protected. That way, they can keep playing—and keep winning! Football helmets have seen many changes over the past 100 years.

Hard leather helmets have straps that keep the skull away from the helmet shell.

The NFL makes helmets required.

Plastic helmets become widespread.

1920s

1930s

1940s

1943

1950s

1953

1955

1960s

1962

Soft leather helmets are used.

Chin straps are used, there are graphics on helmets, and the NFL makes an official move to plastic helmets.

Face masks change to double bar.

The first face mask (single bar) is used.

The first helmet with a radio is created so players and coaches can talk.

The NFL requires face masks.

"Revolution helmets" reduce concussions.

1980s

2000s

Lightweight polycarbonate helmets cushion blows.

2010s to present

1970s

1990s

The air bladder system absorbs more impact.

Face mask grills become popular.

The NFL continually looks for ways to protect league players as well as future generations.

Baseball Specs

DIAMETER
2.86 to 2.94 inches
(7.3–7.5 cm)

LACES THICKNESS
0.1875 inches
(0.4763 cm)

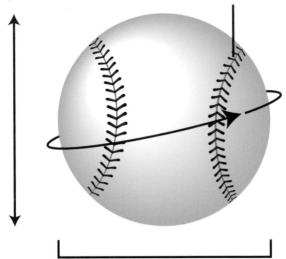

CIRCUMFERENCE
9 to 9.25 inches
(23–23.5 cm)

WEIGHT
5 to 5.25 ounces (142–149 grams)

FAST FACTS

- In the 2016–2017 Major League Baseball (MLB) season, there was a home run surge.
- The laces on the balls used that year were 9% thicker than normal.
- More lace meant more bounce when the ball hit a bat. The ball then flew farther.

2011, Sports Rec

Bouncing Basketballs

Over time, engineers have figured out the perfect amount of air that needs to go into a basketball. Without the right amount, a basketball won't bounce correctly. When a ball has enough air, it bounces just right.

more air in the ball = higher air pressure

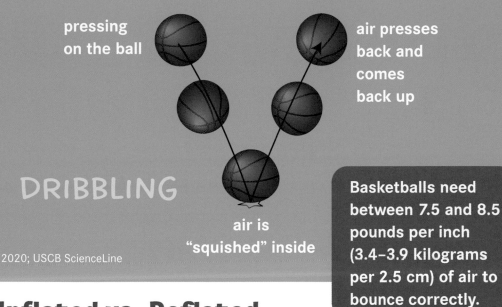

pressing on the ball

air presses back and comes back up

DRIBBLING

air is "squished" inside

2020; USCB ScienceLine

Basketballs need between 7.5 and 8.5 pounds per inch (3.4–3.9 kilograms per 2.5 cm) of air to bounce correctly.

Inflated vs. Deflated

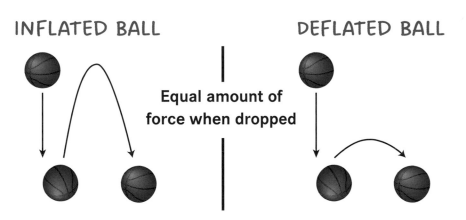

INFLATED BALL

DEFLATED BALL

Equal amount of force when dropped

CHAPTER 2

Better Bodies

Athletes can do amazing things. People still talk about stars from decades ago. Today, athletes can run faster and jump higher. They throw faster and hit harder. Why? New info has helped coaches and athletes. They know how to train and play better. Nutrition is one example. Scientists, sports engineers, coaches, and athletes know about eating well. Engineers have shown that nutrition plays a key role in fueling athletes.

Nutrition Needs of a Basketball Player

PROTEIN

0.6 to 0.8 grams per pound bodyweight (1.4–1.7 g/kg bodyweight)

CARBOHYDRATES

2 to 4.5 grams per pound bodyweight (4.4–10 g/kg bodyweight)

55% of total daily calories

FATS

Remaining daily calories

An athlete wanting to find their macronutrient needs would use the following steps:

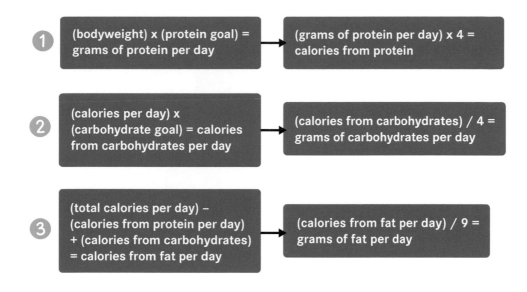

1. (bodyweight) x (protein goal) = grams of protein per day → (grams of protein per day) x 4 = calories from protein

2. (calories per day) x (carbohydrate goal) = calories from carbohydrates per day → (calories from carbohydrates) / 4 = grams of carbohydrates per day

3. (total calories per day) − (calories from protein per day) + (calories from carbohydrates) = calories from fat per day → (calories from fat per day) / 9 = grams of fat per day

2022, Gatorade Sports Science Institute; 2022, Legion

Food for Fuel
Male basketball player weighing 180 pounds (82 kg)

Daily calorie intake: 3,262 calories

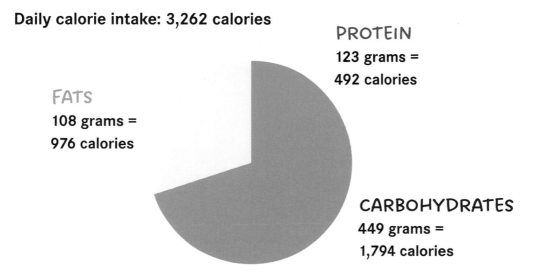

PROTEIN
123 grams =
492 calories

FATS
108 grams =
976 calories

CARBOHYDRATES
449 grams =
1,794 calories

Improvements in Medicine

FAST FACTS

- Sports medicine has gotten better over time, too.
- Advances in surgery have helped athletes. They come back from injuries. They can keep playing for longer.
- Engineered clothing has been approved by doctors. For example, special socks are made with the help of podiatrists. The socks can track how an athlete is playing.

Tommy John Surgery

Tommy John surgery is one of the most common surgeries for athletes. It fixes damage to pitchers' elbows.

90% success rate of Tommy John surgery

82% of MLB pitchers return to the league after surgery

15% of patients experience tears again

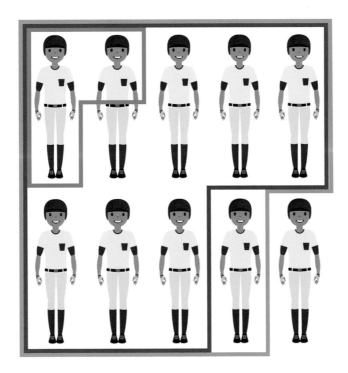

2013, American Journal of Sports Medicine

FAST FACTS

- Weight training helps athletes. It increases how much muscle mass a person has. Pitchers want more muscle mass in their arms. It increases their strength. This can help them throw more strikeouts.

- Resistance training can help balance and coordination. This makes athletes better at their sports.

- Weight and resistance training can also help reduce injuries. Athletes are healthy enough to play longer.

Getting Stronger, Throwing Harder

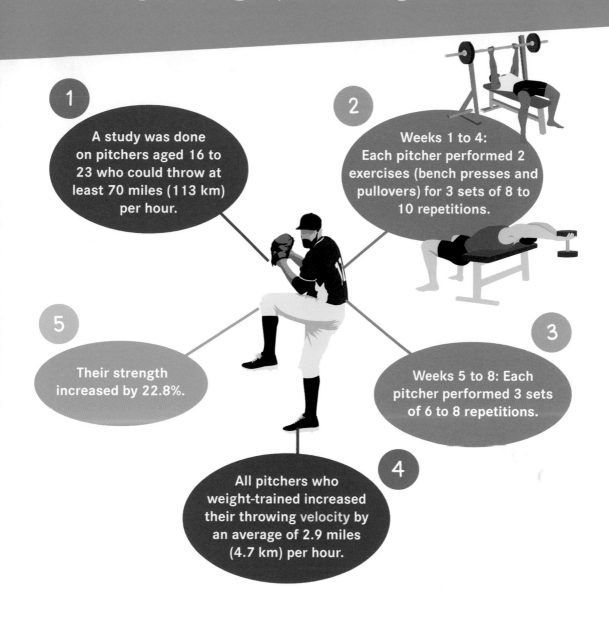

1 A study was done on pitchers aged 16 to 23 who could throw at least 70 miles (113 km) per hour.

2 Weeks 1 to 4: Each pitcher performed 2 exercises (bench presses and pullovers) for 3 sets of 8 to 10 repetitions.

5 Their strength increased by 22.8%.

3 Weeks 5 to 8: Each pitcher performed 3 sets of 6 to 8 repetitions.

4 All pitchers who weight-trained increased their throwing velocity by an average of 2.9 miles (4.7 km) per hour.

2022, Athletic Preparation

CHAPTER 3

Engineered Environments

There are many things that can affect how well athletes play. Some are ones that we might not even think of. Engineers and mathematicians have studied field surface. They study the acoustics of stadiums. They even study air temperature. They want to know how these things impact game play. Some things can help athlete performance a lot. But some things don't. Not all sports engineering leads to more wins.

The Ice Standard

The first indoor hockey game was in Canada in 1875. The rink was made of a sheet of ice. It was 85 feet (26 meters) wide and 200 feet (61 m) long. Engineers have studied ice rinks. They have tried making changes. Olympic ice rinks are now wider. But the 1875 ice remains the standard for National Hockey League rinks!

RINK
200 feet (61 meters) x 85 feet (26 m)

TOP LAYER OF ICE
about 1 inch (2.5 cm) thick

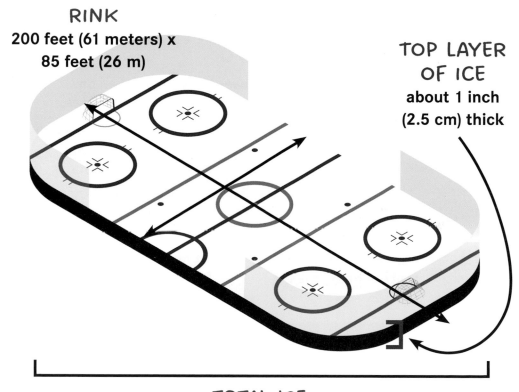

TOTAL ICE
10,600 gallons (40,125 liters) of water

2012, Sports Engine

Turf vs. Grass

Grass used to be the standard. Then turf was engineered. Green plastic is melted into strands. They look like grass. Turf started to replace grass. It is easier to maintain. Turf does not wear down as quickly. It also has a more evenly flat surface to play on. But research has shown that turf is actually more dangerous for players.

28%
higher rate of non-contact lower body injury than on grass. Turf does not absorb impact as well as grass does. It does not have as much "give" as grass.

. . . .

OF THAT POPULATION:

69%
have higher rate of foot/ankle injuries

32%
are at higher risk of knee injuries

16%
increase in lower body injuries on turf than grass

2022, National Football League Players Association

How Warm Air Affects Cyclists

Engineers have figured out how temperature and weather can help an athlete perform better (or worse). Air density tells you how "thick" the air is. At warm temperatures, the air is less dense, or thin. At cold temperatures, the air gets more dense, or thick. Cold, thick air takes more work for an athlete to move through.

Temperature   Air Density

RIDE 1

Temperature:
80°Fahrenheit (27°C)

Air density: thin

Bike speed: 21 miles
(34 km) per hour

Finish time: 28:30

RIDE 2

Temperature:
50°Fahrenheit (10°C)

Air density: thick

Bike speed: 20.7 miles
(33.3 km) per hour

Finish time: 29:00

2022, FitWerx.com

CHAPTER 4

Wonders of Engineering

Breaking records is a hard thing to do. But athletes have better chances of doing so now. They have the help of newer equipment. They have better training programs. And they can wear special gear. Some innovations even help too much. They might create an unfair advantage.

A Record-Setting Olympics

Many swimming records were broken during the 2008 Olympic Games. That is the same year that many top swimmers wore the Speedo LZR swimsuit.

25
total number of records that were broken

When wearing the LZR

23
total number of records that were broken

98
percentage of records that were broken

94
percentage of all swimming races won

2020, Inverse

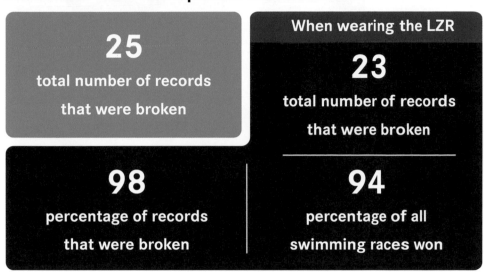

400-meter individual medley

200-meter freestyle

100-meter butterfly

200-meter butterfly

4x100m medley

4x200m freestyle

4x100m freestyle

200-meter medley

Michael Phelps set seven world records and won eight gold medals while wearing the Speedo LZR swimsuit at the 2008 Beijing Olympics.

Running Records

LETESENBET GIDEY
Women's 5,000-meter
14 minutes, 06.62 seconds

JOSHUA CHEPTEGEI
Men's 10,000-meter
26 minutes, 11.00 seconds

FAST FACTS

- In 2020, runner Letesenbet Gidey broke a record. It was for the women's 5,000-meter race.

- That same day, Joshua Cheptegei also broke a record. It was for the men's 10,000-meter race.

- They were both wearing the Nike ZoomX Dragonfly spikes. These shoes were engineered in 2020.

- The superlight shoes have unique foam supports and rigid plates. They help push the wearer forward with each stride. This moves more force forward. The runner's speed increases.

Fastest Marathon

4.5 HOURS
average time it takes to complete a marathon

2 HOURS
considered the shortest amount of time a person needs to complete a marathon

5
percentage of marathon runners who finish in under 3 hours

1 HOUR, 59 MINUTES, 40.2 SECONDS
Eluid Kipchoge's record-breaking unofficial marathon time

In 2019, Eluid Kipchoge ran an unofficial race. He broke the 2-hour marathon record. He did it wearing the Nike Air Zoom Alphafly Next 2 shoes. His shoes were made to improve "bounce" and heel-to-toe drop. Bounce is how much a person moves up and down while running. Too high of a bounce can cause a slower run. Improving a bounce means a runner keeps their bounce height low. This ensures they are moving forward and going faster. Heel-to-toe drop is how thick the heel of the shoe is compared to the toe. Higher heels give runners more cushioning.

2019, ABC News

The Roar of the Crowd

All teams want home field advantage. That is when teams play in their home stadiums. They are more familiar with their field. And they have a lot of fan support. Loud crowds help players feel energetic and ready to win. To increase their home field advantage, some football stadiums are engineered to be extra loud.

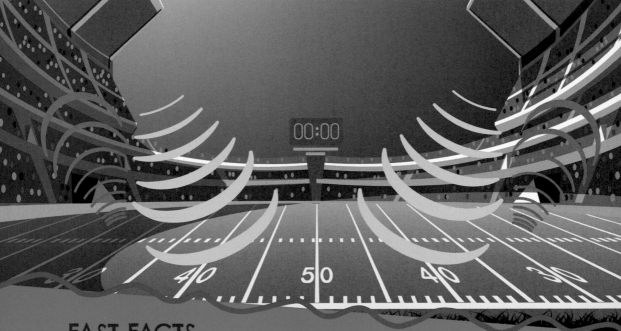

FAST FACTS

- The Seattle Seahawks stadium was designed to be noisy. Other teams have stadiums that were built for this, too.

- Compared to other stadiums, Seattle fans are closer to the field.

- Metal and concrete materials bounce back, rather than absorb, sound. A curved roof aids in louder sound, too. Sound waves reflect off the curved surface.

In 2013, Seattle Seahawks fans set a record for loudest stadium noise level at 137.6 decibels. The Kansas City Chiefs fans broke that record the very next season. They reached 142.2 decibels.

AVERAGE NFL GAME: 95 DECIBELS

2013 SEAHAWKS: 137.6 DECIBELS

0   40   60   80   100   120   140

Top Six Loudest Stadiums

The loudest stadiums have features that help make them so loud. Some have walls that are slightly more curved. Some have concrete or metal that helps sound travel better.

2. LUMEN FIELD
Seattle, Washington
137.6 decibels

4. STATE FARM STADIUM
Glendale, Arizona
130 decibels

2022, NBC Sports

6. U.S. BANK STADIUM
Minneapolis, Minnesota
120 decibels

5. LAMBEAU STADIUM
Green Bay, Wisconsin
123 decibels

1. ARROWHEAD STADIUM
Kansas City, Missouri
142.2 decibels

3. CAESARS SUPERDOME
New Orleans, Louisiana
136.6 decibels

Activity

Improve a Sport

Materials Needed:

- Library or internet access
- Poster board
- Markers or crayons

1. Choose a sport you'd like to improve. Do some research on your sport of choice. What equipment is used? What do athletes wear? Where do they play?

2. Come up with an idea of a way to engineer an improvement to one of the aspects of the sport.

3. Sketch out your idea on poster board. Label the parts. Explain how your changes will improve the sport.

4. Present your idea to your class, friends, or family. Ask them if they have suggestions on ways to improve it even more.

Learn More

Books

Swanson, Jennifer. *The Secret Science of Sports: The Math, Physics, and Mechanical Engineering Behind Every Grand Slam, Triple Axel, and Penalty Kick.* New York: Black Dog & Leventhal, 2021.

Ventura, Marne. *Learning STEM from Basketball: Why Does a Basketball Bounce? And Other Amazing Answers for Kids!* New York: Sky Pony Press, 2021.

Online Resources to Explore with an Adult

Sports Illustrated for Kids: Baseball of Tomorrow: Smarter Equipment

Fun Kids: So What Is Sports Engineering?

Bibliography

Morrison, Jim. "How Speedo Created a Record-Breaking Swimsuit." Scientific American. 2012

Pare, Dustin. "For Better Health, Safety of Athletes Which Playing Surface Is Best?" Global Sports Matter. 2019.

"The Evolution of Technology in Sports." Hire Intelligence. 2022.

Glossary

acoustics (uh-KOO-stiks) the qualities of a room or space that affect how sound travels through it

air pressure (AYR PREH-suhr) the weight of air molecules pressing down on objects

calories (KAL-uh-reez) the amount of energy a certain amount of food gives the body

composite (kom-PAW-sit) made up of many different parts

concussion (kuhn-KUH-shun) an injury to the brain from hitting the head too hard

decibels (DEH-suh-bulz) units of measurement used for sound

drag (DRAG) the force of air pushing against an object in motion

engineering (en-juh-NEER-ing) the work of designing and creating new tools, machines, or buildings

innovations (ih-nuh-VAY-shuns) new creations that advance a field of work

league (LEEG) an organized group of sports teams that play against each other

macronutrient (mah-krow-NOO-tree-uhnt) a type of food your body needs a lot of in order to do work and be healthy

podiatrists (puh-DAI-uh-trists) doctors who work with feet

polycarbonate (paw-lee-KAR-buh-nut) a strong type of plastic

resistance training (ruh-ZIS-tunce TRAY-ning) a form of exercise in which muscles gain strength by pushing against something

shot clock (SHOT KLAHK) a clock that counts down how long teams or players have to try to score

velocity (vuh-LAA-suh-tee) how quickly an object is moving

Index

basketball, 5, 11, 12, 13

Canada, 19

hockey, 19

John, Tommy, 15

Kansas City Chiefs, 27
Kipchoge, Eluid, 25

Major League Baseball (MLB), 10, 15

National Hockey League (NHL), 19
nutrition, 12

Olympic Games, 5, 19, 23

Phelps, Michael, 23

Seattle Seahawks, 26, 27
Speedo LZR, 5, 23

video technology, 6
virtual imaging, 6